D0662664

From:

Date:

Message:

The Power of a
PRAYING®
WOMAN

BOOK of
PRAYERS

STORMIE
OMARTIAN

HARVEST HOUSE PUBLISHERS

EUGENE, OREGON

THE POWER OF A PRAYING® WOMAN BOOK OF PRAYERS
Copyright © 2004 by Stormie Omartian
Published by Harvest House Publishers
Eugene, Oregon 97402
www.harvesthousepublishers.com

ISBN-13: 978-0-7369-1988-3
ISBN-10: 0-7369-1988-0

Printed in the United States of America

08 09 10 11 12 13 14 /VP-KB/ 10 9 8 7 6 5 4

Introduction

There are many things to pray about in our lives, and it is hard to think of all of them. That's why I have found this book of prayers extremely handy to use on a daily basis. It is easy to place the book in a handbag, slip it into a briefcase or place it into a glove compartment. The prayers in this book don't take the place of my own daily prayers, but they get me started. As I pray these prayers they remind me of other things I need to pray about also. I rely on this book of prayers because I can't think of everything, yet I want my life to be thoroughly covered in prayer.

The purpose of this book is to help keep you spiritually anchored and reminded of who you are in the Lord. These prayers will enable you to get closer to God and know Him better. They will be a tool to smooth your path and make your way simple as you ask God to carry the complexities of your life for you. They will keep your mind free from concern over whether you have prayed about important aspects of your situation. These prayers will help you to know whether you are in the center of God's will and fulfilling the purposes He has for you.

~ Stormie Omartian ~

*Those who are planted in the house of the L*ORD
*shall flourish in the courts of our God. They shall
still bear fruit in old age; they shall be fresh and
flourishing, to declare that the L*ORD *is upright.*

— PSALM 92:13-15 —

Lord, Draw Me into a Closer Walk with You

*L*ord, I draw close to You today, grateful that You will draw close to me as You have promised in Your Word (James 4:8). I long to dwell in Your presence, and I want to know You in every way You can be known. Teach me what I need to learn in order to know You better. I don't want to be a person who is "always learning and never able to come to the knowledge of the truth" (2 Timothy 3:7). I want to know the truth about who You are, because I know that You are near to all who call upon You in truth (Psalm 145:18).

I will pray the Father, and He will give you another Helper, that He may abide with you forever—the Spirit of truth, whom the world cannot receive, because it neither sees Him nor knows Him; but you know Him, for He dwells with you and will be in you.

– JOHN 14:16-17 –

Prayer Notes

_____

_____

_____

_____

_____

_____

_____

_____

_____

_____

_____

Lord, Draw Me into a Closer Walk with You

*L*ord, help me to set aside time each day to meet with You alone. As I come before You, teach me to pray the way You want me to. Help me to learn more about You. Lord, You have said, "If anyone thirsts, let him come to Me and drink" (John 7:37). I thirst for more of You because I am in a dry place without You. I come to You this day and drink deeply of Your Spirit. I know You are everywhere, but I also know there are deeper manifestations of Your presence that I long to experience. Draw me close as I draw near to you, so that I may dwell in Your presence like never before.

Draw near to God and He will draw near to you.

— JAMES 4:8 —

Prayer Notes

_____
_____
_____
_____
_____
_____
_____
_____
_____
_____
_____
_____
_____
_____
_____
_____
_____

Lord, Cleanse Me and Make My Heart Right Before You

*L*ord, I come humbly before You and ask You to cleanse my heart and renew a right spirit within me. Forgive me for thoughts I have had, words I have spoken, and things that I have done that are not glorifying to You or are in direct contradiction to Your commands. Specifically, I confess to You (name any thoughts, words, or actions that you know are not pleasing to God). I confess it as sin and I repent of it. I choose to walk away from this pattern of thought or action and live Your way. I know that You are "gracious and merciful, slow to anger and of great kindness" (Joel 2:13). Forgive me for ever taking that for granted.

*If we confess our sins, He is faithful
and just to forgive us our sins and to
cleanse us from all unrighteousness.*

– 1 JOHN 1:9 –

Prayer Notes

_____

_____

_____

_____

_____

_____

_____

_____

_____

_____

_____

_____

_____

Lord, Cleanse Me and Make My Heart Right Before You

*L*ord, I pray that you will "have mercy upon me, O God, according to Your lovingkindness; according to the multitude of Your tender mercies, blot out my transgressions…Create in me a clean heart…and renew a steadfast spirit within me. Do not cast me away from Your presence, and do not take Your Holy Spirit from me" (Psalm 51:1,10-11). "See if there is any wicked way in me, and lead me in the way everlasting" (Psalm 139:24). Show me the truth about myself so that I can see it clearly. Make me clean and right before You. I want to receive Your forgiveness so that times of refreshing may come from Your presence (Acts 3:19).

*I acknowledged my sin to You, and
my iniquity I have not hidden. I said, "I
will confess my transgressions to the LORD,"
and You forgave the iniquity of my sin.*

— PSALM 32:5 —

Prayer Notes

_____

_____

_____

_____

_____

_____

_____

_____

_____

_____

_____

_____

_____

Lord, Help Me to Be a Forgiving Person

*L*ord, help me to be a forgiving person. Show me where I am not. If I have any anger, bitterness, resentment, or unforgiveness that I am not recognizing, reveal it to me and I will confess it to You as sin. Specifically, I ask You to help me fully forgive (name anyone you feel you need to forgive). Make me to understand the depth of Your forgiveness toward me so that I won't hold back forgiveness from others. I realize that my forgiving someone doesn't make them right; it makes me free. I also realize that You are the only one who knows the whole story, and You will see justice done.

The discretion of a man makes him slow to anger, and his glory is to overlook a transgression.

– PROVERBS 19:11 –

Prayer Notes

_____

_____

_____

_____

_____

_____

_____

_____

_____

_____

_____

_____

_____

_____

Lord, Help Me to Be a Forgiving Person

*L*ord, I don't want anything to come between You and me, and I don't want my prayers to be hindered because I have entertained sin in my heart. I choose this day to forgive everyone and everything, and walk free from the death that unforgiveness brings. If any person has unforgiveness toward me, I pray You would soften their heart to forgive me and show me what I can do to help resolve this issue between us. I know that I cannot be a light to others as long as I am walking in the darkness of unforgiveness. I choose to walk in the light as You are in the light and be cleansed from all sin (1 John 1:7).

Judge not, and you shall not be judged.
Condemn not, and you shall not be
condemned. Forgive, and you will be forgiven.
— LUKE 6:37 —

Prayer Notes

_____
_____
_____
_____
_____
_____
_____
_____
_____
_____
_____
_____
_____
_____

Lord, Teach Me to Walk in Obedience to Your Ways

*L*ord, Your Word says that those of us who love Your law will have great peace and nothing will cause us to stumble (Psalm 119:165). I love Your law because I know it is good and it is there for my benefit. Enable me to live in obedience to each part of it so that I will not stumble and fall. Help me to obey You so that I can dwell in the confidence and peace of knowing I am living Your way. My heart wants to obey You in all things, Lord. Please show me where I am not doing that. "With my whole heart I have sought You; oh, let me not wander from Your commandments!" (Psalm 119:10).

He who has My commandments and
keeps them, it is he who loves Me. And he
who loves Me will be loved by My Father,
and I will love him and manifest Myself to him.

– JOHN 14:21 –

Prayer Notes

_____
_____
_____
_____
_____
_____
_____
_____
_____
_____
_____
_____
_____

Lord, Teach Me to Walk in Obedience to Your Ways

Lord, Your Word says that "if we say we have no sin, we deceive ourselves, and the truth is not in us" (1 John 1:8). I don't want to deceive myself by not asking You where I am missing the mark You have set for my life. Show me if I'm doing things I should not. Help me to hear Your specific instructions to me. Speak to me clearly through Your Word so I will know what's right and what's wrong. I don't want to grieve the Holy Spirit in anything I do (Ephesians 4:30). Help me to be ever learning about Your ways so I can live in the fullness of Your presence and move into all You have for me.

He who keeps His commandments abides in Him,
and He in him. And by this we know that He
abides in us, by the Spirit whom He has given us.

— 1 JOHN 3:24 —

Prayer Notes

_____

_____

_____

_____

_____

_____

_____

_____

_____

_____

_____

_____

_____

_____

Lord, Strengthen Me to Stand Against the Enemy

*L*ord, I thank You for suffering and dying on the cross for me, and for rising again to defeat death and hell. My enemy is defeated because of what You have done. Thank You that You have given me all authority over him (Luke 10:19). Show me when I am not recognizing the encroachment of the enemy in my life. Teach me to use that authority You have given me to see him defeated in every area. Help me to fast and pray regularly in order to break any stronghold the enemy is trying to erect in my life. By the power of Your Holy Spirit I can successfully resist the devil and he must flee from me (James 4:7).

Be strong in the Lord and in the power of His might. Put on the whole armor of God, that you may be able to stand against the wiles of the devil.

— Ephesians 6:10-11 —

Prayer Notes

_____

_____

_____

_____

_____

_____

_____

_____

_____

_____

_____

_____

_____

_____

_____

Lord, Strengthen Me to Stand Against the Enemy

Lord, I know in the midst of the battle I don't have to be afraid in the face of the enemy (Deuteronomy 20:3). Thank you that even though the enemy tries to take me captive to do his will, You have given me the power to escape his snares completely (2 Timothy 2:26). Thank You that You are my shield because I live Your way (Proverbs 2:7). Help me to "not be overcome by evil," but instead give me the strength to "overcome evil with good" (Romans 12:21). Hide me in the secret place of Your presence from the plots of evil men (Psalm 31:20). The enemy will never bring me down as long as I stand strong in You.

When the whirlwind passes by, the wicked is no more, but the righteous has an everlasting foundation.

— PROVERBS 10:25 —

Prayer Notes

_____

_____

_____

_____

_____

_____

_____

_____

_____

_____

_____

_____

_____

_____

Lord, Show Me How to Take Control of My Mind

*L*ord, I don't ever want to walk according to my own thinking (Isaiah 65:2). I want to bring every thought captive and control my mind. Your Word is "a discerner of the thoughts and intents of the heart" (Hebrews 4:12). As I read Your Word, may it reveal any wrong thinking in me. May Your Word be so etched in my mind that I will be able to identify a lie of the enemy the minute I hear it. Spirit of truth, keep me undeceived. I know You have given me authority "over all the power of the enemy" (Luke 10:19), and so I command the enemy to get away from my mind. I refuse to listen to lies.

*Be renewed in the spirit of
your mind, and…put on the new
man which was created according to
God, in true righteousness and holiness.*

— EPHESIANS 4:23-24 —

Prayer Notes

_____

_____

_____

_____

_____

_____

_____

_____

_____

_____

_____

_____

_____

_____

Lord, Show Me How to Take Control of My Mind

*L*ord, I don't want to think futile and foolish thoughts or give place to thoughts that are not glorifying to You (Romans 1:21). Thank You that I "have the mind of Christ" (1 Corinthians 2:16). I want Your thoughts to be my thoughts. Show me where I have filled my mind with anything that is ungodly. Help me to resist doing that and instead fill my mind with thoughts, words, music, and images that are glorifying to You. Help me to think upon what is true, noble, just, pure, lovely, of good report, virtuous, and praiseworthy (Philippians 4:8). I lay claim to the "sound mind" that You have given me (2 Timothy 1:7).

*Do not be conformed to this world, but
be transformed by the renewing of your
mind, that you may prove what is that good
and acceptable and perfect will of God.*

– ROMANS 12:2 –

Prayer Notes

_____
_____
_____
_____
_____
_____
_____
_____
_____
_____
_____
_____
_____
_____

Lord, Rule Me in Every Area of My Life

*L*ord, I bow before You this day and declare that You are Lord over every area of my life. I surrender myself and my life to You and invite You to rule in every part of my mind, soul, body and spirit. I love You with all my heart, with all my soul, and with all my mind. I commit to trusting You with my whole being. Enable me to deny myself in order to take up my cross daily and follow you (Luke 9:23). I want to be Your disciple just as You have said in Your Word (Luke 14:27). I want to lose my life in You so I can save it (Luke 9:24).

*If we live, we live to the Lord; and if
we die, we die to the Lord. Therefore,
whether we live or die, we are the Lord's.*

— ROMANS 14:8 —

Prayer Notes

Lord, Rule Me in Every Area of My Life

Lord, my desire is to please You and hold nothing back. I surrender my relationships, my finances, my work, my recreation, my decisions, my time, my body, my mind, my soul, my desires, and my dreams. I put them all in Your hands to be used for Your glory. I declare this day that "I have been crucified with Christ; it is no longer I who live, but Christ lives in me; and the life which I now live in the flesh I live by faith in the Son of God, who loved me and gave Himself for me" (Galatians 2:20). Rule me in every area of my life, Lord, and lead me into all that You have for me.

*As you have therefore received Christ Jesus
the Lord, so walk in Him, rooted and built up
in Him and established in the faith, as you have
been taught, abounding in it with thanksgiving.*

– Colossians 2:6-7 –

Prayer Notes

Lord, Take Me Deeper in Your Word

*L*ord, "Your Word is a lamp to my feet and a light to my path" (Psalm 119:105). Enable me to truly comprehend its deepest meaning. Give me greater understanding than I have ever had before, and reveal to me the hidden treasures buried there. I pray that I will have a heart that is teachable and open to what You want me to know. Change me as I read it. Help me to be diligent to put Your Word inside my soul faithfully every day. Show me where I'm wasting time that could be better spent reading Your Word. Give me the ability to memorize it. Etch it in my mind and heart so that it becomes a part of me.

He who looks into the perfect law of liberty and continues in it, and is not a forgetful hearer but a doer of the work, this one will be blessed in what he does.

— JAMES 1:25 —

Prayer Notes

_____
_____
_____
_____
_____
_____
_____
_____
_____
_____
_____
_____

Lord, Take Me Deeper in Your Word

Lord, may Your Word remind me of who You are and how much You love me. May it bring the security of knowing my life is in Your hands and You will supply all my needs. Thank You, Lord, that when I look into Your Word I find You. Give me ears to recognize Your voice speaking to me every time I read it (Mark 4:23). When I hear Your voice and follow You, my life is full. When I get off the path You have for me, my life is empty. Guide, perfect, and fill me with Your Word this day.

*Blessed is the man who walks not in the
counsel of the ungodly, nor stands in the path
of sinners, nor sits in the seat of the scornful; but
his delight is in the law of the Lord, and in His
law he meditates day and night. He shall be like
a tree planted by the rivers of water that brings
forth its fruit in its season, whose leaf also shall not
wither; and whatever he does shall prosper.*

— Psalm 1:1-3 —

Prayer Notes

_____

_____

_____

_____

_____

_____

_____

_____

_____

Lord, Instruct Me as I Put My Life in Right Order

Lord, I pray You would help me set my life in right order. I want to always put You first above all else in my life. Teach me how to love You with all my heart, mind, and soul. Show me when I am not doing that. Show me if I have lifted up my soul to an idol. My desire is to serve You and only You. Please help me to live accordingly. Give me a submissive heart. Help me to always submit to the governing authorities and the correct people in my family, work, and church. Show me who the proper spiritual authorities are to be in my life. Plant me in the church You want me to be in.

Obey those who rule over you, and be submissive,
for they watch out for your souls, as those who must
give account. Let them do so with joy and not with
grief, for that would be unprofitable for you.

– HEBREWS 13:17 –

Prayer Notes

Lord, Instruct Me as I Put My Life in Right Order

Lord, help me to willingly submit myself to others where I need to do so. Show me clearly to whom I am to be submitted and how I am to do it. Give me discernment and wisdom about this. Show me any time I am not submitted to the right people in the right way. I know that if my life is not in proper order I will not receive the blessings You have for me. But I also know that if I seek You first, all that I need will be added to me (Matthew 6:33). I seek You first this day and ask that You would enable me to put my life in perfect order.

He who finds his life will lose it, and he who loses his life for My sake will find it.

– MATTHEW 10:39 –

Prayer Notes

_____

_____

_____

_____

_____

_____

_____

_____

_____

_____

_____

_____

_____

_____

_____

_____

Lord, Prepare Me to Be a True Worshiper

Lord, there is no source of greater joy for me than worshiping You. I come into Your presence with thanksgiving and bow before You this day. I exalt Your name, for You are great and worthy to be praised. "You have put gladness in my heart" (Psalm 4:7). All honor and majesty, strength and glory, holiness and righteousness are Yours, O Lord. You are "gracious and full of compassion, slow to anger and great in mercy" (Psalm 145:8). You are "mighty in power" and Your "understanding is infinite" (Psalm 147:5). You give food to the hungry and freedom to the prisoners. Thank You that You open the eyes of the blind and raise up those who are bowed down (Psalm 146:7-8).

Whoever offers praise glorifies Me;
and to him who orders his conduct
aright I will show the salvation of God.

— PSALM 50:23 —

Prayer Notes

_____

_____

_____

_____

_____

_____

_____

_____

_____

_____

_____

_____

_____

_____

_____

Lord, Prepare Me to Be a True Worshiper

Lord, teach me to worship You with my whole heart the way You want me to. Make me a true worshiper. May praise and worship of You be my first response to every circumstance. I praise Your name this day, Lord, for You are good and Your mercy endures forever (Psalm 136:1). "Because Your lovingkindness is better than life, my lips shall praise You. Thus I will bless You while I live; I will lift up my hands in Your name" (Psalm 63:3-4). I will declare Your "glory among the nations" and Your "wonders among all peoples" (Psalm 96:3). I worship You in the splendor of Your holiness and give You the glory due Your name (Psalm 29:2).

*I will worship toward Your holy
temple, and praise Your name for Your
lovingkindness and Your truth; for You have
magnified Your word above all Your name.*

— PSALM 138:2 —

Prayer Notes

Lord, Bless Me in the Work I Do

Lord, I pray You would show me what work I am supposed to be doing. If it is something other than what I am doing now, reveal it to me. If it is something I am to do in addition to what I am already doing, show me that too. Whatever it is You have called me to do, both now and in the future, I pray You will give me the strength and energy to get it done well. May I find great fulfillment and satisfaction in every aspect of it, even the most difficult and unpleasant parts. Thank You that in all labor there is profit of one kind or another (Proverbs 14:23).

Blessed is every one who fears the Lord, who walks in His ways. When you eat the labor of your hands, you shall be happy, and it shall be well with you.

— PSALM 128:1-2 —

Prayer Notes

_____

_____

_____

_____

_____

_____

_____

_____

_____

_____

_____

_____

_____

Lord, Bless Me in the Work I Do

Lord, I thank You for the abilities You have given me. Where I am lacking in skill help me to grow and improve so that I do my work well. Open doors of opportunity to use my skills and close doors that I am not to go through. Give me wisdom and direction about that. I commit my work to You, Lord, knowing You will establish it (Proverbs 16:3). May it always be that I love the work I do and be able to do the work I love. Establish the work of my hands so that what I do will find favor with others and be a blessing for many. May it always be glorifying to You.

*Let the beauty of the LORD our God be
upon us, and establish the work of our hands
for us; yes, establish the work of our hands.*

– PSALM 90:17 –

Prayer Notes

Lord, Plant Me so I Will Bear the Fruit of Your Spirit

Lord, I pray You would plant the fruit of Your Spirit in me and cause it to flourish. Help me to abide in You, Jesus, so that I will bear fruit in my life. Holy Spirit, fill me afresh with Your love today so that it will flow out of me and into the lives of others. You said in Your Word to "let the peace of Christ rule in your hearts" (Colossians 3:15). I pray that Your peace would rule my heart and mind to such a degree that people would sense it when they are around me. Help me to "pursue the things which make for peace and the things by which one may edify another" (Romans 14:19).

The fruit of the Spirit is love, joy, peace,
longsuffering, kindness, goodness,
faithfulness, gentleness, self-control.
Against such there is no law.

— GALATIANS 5:22-23 —

Prayer Notes

_____

_____

_____

_____

_____

_____

_____

_____

_____

_____

_____

_____

_____

Lord, Plant Me so I Will Bear the Fruit of Your Spirit

*L*ord, where I need to be pruned in order to bear more fruit, I submit myself to You. I know that without You I can do nothing. You are the vine and I am the branch. I must abide in You in order to bear fruit. Thank You for Your promise that if I abide in You and Your Word abides in me, I can ask what I desire and it will be done for me (John 15:7). Thank You for Your promise that says if I ask I will receive (John 16:24). May I be like a tree planted by the rivers of Your living water so that I will bring forth fruit in season that won't wither (Psalm 1:3).

By this My Father is glorified, that you
bear much fruit; so you will be My disciples.

Prayer Notes

_____
_____
_____
_____
_____
_____
_____
_____
_____
_____
_____
_____
_____
_____
_____

Lord, Preserve Me in Purity and Holiness

Lord, You have said in Your Word that You did not call me to uncleanness, but in holiness (1 Thessalonians 4:7). You chose me to be holy and blameless before You. I know that I have been washed clean and made holy by the blood of Jesus (1 Corinthians 6:11). You have clothed me in Your righteousness and enabled me to put on the new man "in true righteousness and holiness" (Ephesians 4:24). Help me to "cling to what is good" (Romans 12:9) and keep myself pure (1 Timothy 5:22). Lord, help me to separate myself from anything that is not holy. I don't want to waste my life on things that have no value.

*He chose us in Him before the foundation
of the world, that we should be holy and
without blame before Him in love.*

— Ephesians 1:4 —

Prayer Notes

Lord, Preserve Me in Purity and Holiness

*L*ord, help me to examine my ways so that I can return to Your ways wherever I have strayed. Enable me to take any steps necessary in order to be pure before You. I want to be holy as You are holy. Make me a partaker of Your holiness (Hebrews 12:10), and may my spirit, soul, and body be kept blameless (1 Thessalonians 5:23). I know that You have called me to purity and holiness, and You have said that "He who calls you is faithful, who will also do it" (1 Thessalonians 5:24). Thank You that You will keep me pure and holy so I will be fully prepared for all You have for me.

Blessed are the pure in heart, for they shall see God.
— MATTHEW 5:8 —

Prayer Notes

_____
_____
_____
_____
_____
_____
_____
_____
_____
_____
_____
_____
_____
_____
_____
_____
_____

Lord, Move Me into the Purpose for Which I Was Created

*L*ord, I know Your plan for me existed before I knew You, and You will bring it to pass. Help me to "walk worthy of the calling with which [I was] called" (Ephesians 4:1). I know there is an appointed plan for me, and I have a destiny that will now be fulfilled. Help me to live my life with a sense of purpose and understanding of the calling You have given me. Take away any discouragement I may feel and replace it with joyful anticipation of what You are going to do through me. Use me as Your instrument to make a positive difference in the lives of those whom You put in my path.

*Be even more diligent to make your
call and election sure, for if you do
these things you will never stumble.*

— 2 PETER 1:10 —

Prayer Notes

_____

_____

_____

_____

_____

_____

_____

_____

_____

_____

_____

_____

_____

_____

Lord, Move Me into the Purpose for Which I Was Created

Lord, give me a vision for my life. I put my identity in You and my destiny in Your hands. Show me if what I am doing now is what I am supposed to be doing. I want what You are building in my life to last for eternity. I know that "all things work together for good" to those who love You and are called according to Your purpose (Romans 8:28). I pray that You would show me clearly what the gifts and talents are that You have placed in me. Lead me in the way I should go as I grow in them. Enable me to use them according to Your will and for Your glory.

*In Him also we have obtained
an inheritance, being predestined
according to the purpose of Him who works
all things according to the counsel of His will.*
— Ephesians 1:11 —

Prayer Notes

Lord, Guide Me in All My Relationships

Lord, I lift up every one of my relationships to You and ask You to bless them. I ask that Your peace would reign in them and that each one would be glorifying to You. Help me to choose my friends wisely so I won't be lead astray. Give me discernment and strength to separate myself from anyone who is not a good influence. I release all my relationships to You and pray that Your will be done in each one of them. I especially pray for my relationship with each of my family members. I pray You would bring healing, reconciliation, and restoration where it is needed. Bless these relationships and make them strong.

*God sets the solitary in families; He brings
out those who are bound into prosperity.*

— PSALM 68:6 —

Prayer Notes

Lord, Guide Me in All My Relationships

Lord, I pray for any relationships I have with people who don't know You. Give me words to say that will turn their hearts toward You. Help me to be Your light to them. Specifically, I pray for (name an unbeliever or someone who has walked away from God). Soften this person's heart to open her (his) eyes to receive You and follow You faithfully. I also pray for godly friends, role models, and mentors to come into my life. Send people who will speak the truth in love. I pray especially that there will be women in my life who are trustworthy, kind, loving, and faithful. May we mutually raise the standards to which we aspire.

Let all bitterness, wrath, anger,
clamor, and evil speaking be put away
from you, with all malice. And be kind
to one another, tenderhearted, forgiving
one another, just as God in Christ forgave you.

– EPHESIANS 4:31-32 –

Prayer Notes

_____

_____

_____

_____

_____

_____

_____

_____

_____

_____

_____

_____

_____

Lord, Keep Me in the Center of Your Will

*L*ord, guide my every step. Lead me "in Your righteousness" and "make Your way straight before my face" (Psalm 5:8). As I draw close and walk in intimate relationship with You each day, I pray You will get me where I need to go. Even as Jesus said, "Not My will, but Yours, be done" (Luke 22:42), so I say to You, not *my* will but *Your* will be done in my life. "I delight to do Your will, O my God" (Psalm 40:8). You are more important to me than anything. Your will is more important to me than my desires. I want to live as Your servant, doing Your will from my heart (Ephesians 6:6).

Not everyone who says to Me, "Lord, Lord,"
shall enter the kingdom of heaven, but he
who does the will of My Father in heaven.

— MATTHEW 7:21 —

Prayer Notes

_____

_____

_____

_____

_____

_____

_____

_____

_____

_____

_____

_____

_____

Lord, Keep Me in the Center of Your Will

Lord, help me to hear Your voice saying, "This is the way, walk in it." Speak to me from Your Word so that I will have understanding. Show me any area of my life where I am not right on target. If there is something I should be doing, reveal it to me so that I can correct my course. I want to do only what You want me to do and go only where You want me to go. I know we are not to direct our own steps (Jeremiah 10:23). I want to move into all You have for me and become all You made me to be by walking in Your perfect will for my life now.

You have need of endurance, so that after you have done the will of God, you may receive the promise.

— HEBREWS 10:36 —

Prayer Notes

_____

_____

_____

_____

_____

_____

_____

_____

_____

_____

_____

_____

_____

_____

_____

_____

Lord, Protect Me and All I Care About

Lord, I pray for Your hand of protection to be upon me. I trust in Your Word, which assures me that You are my rock, my fortress, my deliverer, my shield, my stronghold, and my strength in whom I trust. I want to dwell in Your secret place and abide in Your shadow (Psalm 91:1). Keep me under the umbrella of Your protection. Help me never to stray from the center of Your will or off the path You have for me. Enable me to always hear Your voice guiding me. Send Your angels to keep charge over me and keep me in all my ways. May they bear me up, so that I will not even stumble (Psalm 91:12).

Because you have made the LORD, who
is my refuge, even the Most High, your
dwelling place, no evil shall befall you,
nor shall any plague come near your dwelling.

— PSALM 91:9-10 —

Prayer Notes

_____
_____
_____
_____
_____
_____
_____
_____
_____
_____
_____
_____
_____
_____

Lord, Protect Me and All I Care About

Lord, You are my refuge and strength and "a very present help in trouble." Therefore I will not fear, "even though the earth be removed and though the mountains be carried to the midst of the sea" (Psalm 46:1-2). Protect me from the plans of evil people, and keep me from sudden danger. "Be merciful to me, O God, be merciful to me! For my soul trusts in You; and in the shadow of Your wings I will make my refuge" (Psalm 57:1). Thank You that "I will both lie down in peace, and sleep; for You alone, O LORD, make me dwell in safety" (Psalm 4:8). Thank You for Your promises of protection.

When you pass through the waters, I will be with you; and through the rivers, they shall not overflow you. When you walk through the fire, you shall not be burned, nor shall the flame scorch you.

— ISAIAH 43:2 —

Prayer Notes

Lord, Give Me Wisdom to Make Right Decisions

*L*ord, I pray You would give me Your wisdom and understanding in all things. I know wisdom is better than gold and understanding better than silver (Proverbs 16:16), so make me rich in wisdom and wealthy in understanding. Thank You that You give "wisdom to the wise and knowledge to those who have understanding" (Daniel 2:21). Increase my wisdom and knowledge so I can see Your truth in every situation. Give me discernment for each decision I must make. Please help me to always seek godly counsel and not look to the world and ungodly people for answers. Thank You, Lord, that You will give me the counsel and instruction I need, even as I sleep.

The mouth of the righteous speaks wisdom,
and his tongue talks of justice. The law of his
God is in his heart; none of his steps shall slide.

— PSALM 37:30-31 —

Prayer Notes

Lord, Give Me Wisdom to Make Right Decisions

Lord, You said in Your Word that You store up sound wisdom for the upright (Proverbs 2:7). Help me to walk uprightly, righteously, and obediently to Your commands. May I never be wise in my own eyes, but may I always fear You. Keep me far from evil so that I can claim the health and strength Your Word promises (Proverbs 3:7-8). Give me the wisdom, knowledge, understanding, direction, and discernment I need to keep me away from the plans of evil so that I will walk safely and not stumble (Proverbs 2:10-13). Lord, I know that in You "are hidden all the treasures of wisdom and knowledge" (Colossians 2:3). Help me to discover those treasures.

Through wisdom a house is built, and by under-
standing it is established; by knowledge the rooms
are filled with all precious and pleasant riches.

— PROVERBS 24:3-4 —

Prayer Notes

Lord, Deliver Me from Every Evil Work

Lord, thank You that You have promised to "deliver me from every evil work and preserve me" for Your heavenly kingdom (2 Timothy 4:18). I know that "we do not wrestle against flesh and blood, but against principalities, against powers, against the rulers of the darkness of this age, against spiritual hosts of wickedness in the heavenly places" (Ephesians 6:12). Thank You that You have put all these enemies under Your feet (Ephesians 1:22), and "there is nothing covered that will not be revealed, and hidden that will not be known" (Matthew 10:26). "My times are in Your hand; deliver me from the hand of my enemies, and from those who persecute me" (Psalm 31:15).

Because he has set his love upon Me,
therefore I will deliver him, I will set him
on high, because he has known My name.

— Psalm 91:14 —

Prayer Notes

_____

_____

_____

_____

_____

_____

_____

_____

_____

_____

_____

_____

_____

_____

Lord, Deliver Me from Every Evil Work

Lord, I ask that You would deliver me from anything that binds me or separates me from You. I specifically ask to be delivered from (name a specific area where you want to be set free). Where I have opened the door for the enemy with my own desires, I repent of that. In Jesus' name, I pray that every stronghold erected around me by the enemy will be brought down to nothing. Make darkness light before me and the crooked places straight (Isaiah 42:16). I know that You who have begun a good work in me will complete it (Philippians 1:6). Give me patience to not give up and the strength to stand strong in Your Word.

Call upon Me in the day of trouble; I
will deliver you, and you shall glorify Me.

— PSALM 50:15 —

Prayer Notes

_____
_____
_____
_____
_____
_____
_____
_____
_____
_____
_____
_____
_____
_____
_____
_____

Lord, Set Me Free from Negative Emotions

Lord, help me to live in Your joy and peace. Give me strength and understanding to resist anxiety, anger, envy, depression, bitterness, hopelessness, loneliness, fear, and guilt. Rescue me when "my spirit is overwhelmed within me; my heart within me is distressed" (Psalm 143:4). I refuse to let my life be brought down by negative emotions such as these. When I am tempted to give in to them, show me Your truth. You have said in Your Word that by our patience we can possess our souls (Luke 21:19). Give me patience so I can do that. Help me to keep my "heart with all diligence," for I know that "out of it spring the issues of life" (Proverbs 4:23).

The righteous cry out, and the
LORD hears, and delivers them out
of all their troubles. The LORD is near
to those who have a broken heart, and
saves such as have a contrite spirit.

— PSALM 34:17-18 —

Prayer Notes

Lord, Set Me Free from Negative Emotions

Lord, help me to not be insecure and self-focused so that I miss opportunities to focus on You and extend Your love. May I be sensitive to the needs, trials, and weaknesses of others and not overly sensitive to myself. What You accomplished on the cross is my source of greatest joy. Help me to concentrate on that. Thank You, Lord, that in my distress I can call on You. "Cause me to hear Your lovingkindness in the morning, for in You do I trust; cause me to know the way in which I should walk, for I lift up my soul to You" (Psalm 143:8). May the joy of knowing You fill my heart with happiness and peace.

*Be anxious for nothing, but in everything by prayer
and supplication, with thanksgiving, let your
requests be made known to God; and the peace of
God, which surpasses all understanding, will guard
your hearts and minds through Christ Jesus.*

— PHILIPPIANS 4:6-7 —

Prayer Notes

_____

_____

_____

_____

_____

_____

_____

_____

_____

_____

_____

_____

Lord, Comfort Me in Times of Trouble

Lord, help me remember that no matter how dark my situation may become, You are the light of my life and can never be put out. No matter what dark clouds settle on my life, You will lift me above the storm and into the comfort of Your presence. Only You can take whatever loss I experience and fill that empty place with good. Only You can take away my grief and pain and dry my tears. "Hear me when I call, O God of my righteousness! You have relieved me in my distress; have mercy on me, and hear my prayer" (Psalm 4:1). I want to stand strong in Your truth and not be swept away by my emotions.

Blessed are the poor in spirit, for theirs is the kingdom of heaven. Blessed are those who mourn, for they shall be comforted.

– MATTHEW 5:3-4 –

Prayer Notes

Lord, Comfort Me in Times of Trouble

*L*ord, help me remember to give thanks to You in all things, knowing that You reign in the midst of them. I know when I pass through the waters You will be with me and the river will not overflow me. When I walk through the fire I will not be burned, nor will the flame touch me (Isaiah 43:1-2). I pray that You, O God of hope, will fill me with all joy and peace and faith so that I will "abound in hope by the power of the Holy Spirit" (Romans 15:13). Thank You that You have sent Your Holy Spirit to be my Comforter and Helper. Please remind me of that in the midst of difficult times.

May the God of all grace, who called
us to His eternal glory by Christ Jesus,
after you have suffered a while, perfect,
establish, strengthen, and settle you.

– 1 PETER 5:10 –

Prayer Notes

_____

_____

_____

_____

_____

_____

_____

_____

_____

_____

_____

_____

Lord, Enable Me to Resist the Temptation to Sin

Lord, do not allow me to be led into temptation, but deliver me from the evil one and his plans for my downfall. In the name of Jesus, I break any hold temptation has on me. Keep me strong and able to resist anything that would tempt me away from all You have for me. I pray I will have no secret thoughts where I entertain ungodly desires to do or say something I shouldn't. I pray that I will have no secret life where I do things I would be ashamed to have others see. I don't want to have fellowship with unfruitful works of darkness. Help me, instead, to expose them (Ephesians 5:11).

*Blessed is the man who endures
temptation; for when he has been approved,
he will receive the crown of life which the
Lord has promised to those who love Him.*

— JAMES 1:12 —

Prayer Notes

_____

_____

_____

_____

_____

_____

_____

_____

_____

_____

_____

_____

_____

Lord, Enable Me to Resist the Temptation to Sin

*L*ord, help me to hide Your Word in my heart so I will see clearly and not sin against You in any way (Psalm 119:11). Thank You, Lord, that You are near to all who call upon You, and You will fulfill the desire of those who fear You. Thank You that You hear my cries and will save me from any weakness that could lead me away from all You have for me (Psalm 145:18-19). Thank You that You know "how to deliver the godly out of temptations" (2 Peter 2:9). Thank You that You will deliver me out of all temptation and keep it far from me.

No temptation has overtaken you except such
as is common to man; but God is faithful, who
will not allow you to be tempted beyond what you
are able, but with the temptation will also make
the way of escape, that you may be able to bear it.

– 1 CORINTHIANS 10:13 –

Prayer Notes

Lord, Heal Me and Help Me Care for My Body

Lord, I thank You that You are the Healer. I look to You for my healing whenever I am injured or sick. I pray that You would strengthen and heal me today. Specifically, I pray for (name any area where you need the Lord to heal you). Heal me "that it might be fulfilled which was spoken by Isaiah the prophet, saying: 'He Himself took our infirmities and bore our sicknesses'" (Matthew 8:17). You suffered, died, and were buried for me so that I might have healing, forgiveness, and eternal life. By Your stripes, I am healed (1 Peter 2:24). In Your presence I can reach out and touch You and in turn be touched by You.

*Heal me, O LORD, and I shall be healed; save
me, and I shall be saved, for You are my praise.*
— JEREMIAH 17:14 —

Prayer Notes

Lord, Heal Me and Help Me Care for My Body

Lord, I want everything I do to be glorifying to You. Help me to be a good steward of the body You have given me. Teach me and help me learn. Lead me to people who can help or advise me. When I am sick and need to see a doctor, show me which doctor to see and give that doctor wisdom as to how to treat me. Enable me to discipline my body and bring it into subjection (1 Corinthians 9:27). I know that my body is the temple of Your Holy Spirit, who dwells in me. Help me to fully understand this truth so that I will keep my temple clean and healthy.

Therefore, whether you eat or drink, or whatever you do, do all to the glory of God.

— 1 CORINTHIANS 10:31 —

Prayer Notes

_____

_____

_____

_____

_____

_____

_____

_____

_____

_____

_____

_____

_____

_____

_____

_____

_____

Lord, Free Me from Ungodly Fear

Lord, You are my light and my salvation. You are the strength of my life. Of whom, then, shall I be afraid? (Psalm 27:1). I will be strong and of good courage, for I know You are with me wherever I go (Joshua 1:9). Free me from all ungodly fear, for I know fear is never of You. I pray You would guard my heart and mind from the spirit of fear. If I experience feelings of fear, I pray You would replace them with Your perfect love. If I have gotten my mind off of You and on my circumstances, help me to reverse that process so that my mind is off my circumstances and on You.

God has not given us a spirit of fear, but
of power and of love and of a sound mind.

– 2 TIMOTHY 1:7 –

Prayer Notes

_____

_____

_____

_____

_____

_____

_____

_____

_____

_____

_____

_____

_____

_____

_____

_____

Lord, Free Me from Ungodly Fear

Lord, Your Word says that You will put fear in the hearts of Your people and You will not turn away from doing them good (Jeremiah 32:40). I pray You would do that for me. I know that You have not given me a spirit of fear, so I reject that and instead claim the power, love, and sound mind You have for me. "Oh, how great is Your goodness, which You have laid up for those who fear You" (Psalm 31:19). Because I have received a kingdom that cannot be shaken, may I have grace by which to serve You acceptably with reverence and godly fear all the days of my life (Hebrews 12:28).

Teach me Your way, O LORD; I will walk in
Your truth; unite my heart to fear Your name.
— PSALM 86:11 —

Prayer Notes

Lord, Use Me to Touch the Lives of Others

Lord, help me to serve You the way You want me to. Reveal to me any area of my life where I should be giving to someone right now. Open my eyes to see the need. Give me a generous heart to give to the poor. Help me to be a good steward of the blessings You have given me by sharing what I have with others. Show me whom You want me to extend my hand to at this time. Fill me with Your love for all people, and help me to communicate it in a way that can be clearly perceived. Use me to touch the lives of others with the hope that is in me.

*By this we know love, because He laid
down His life for us. And we also ought
to lay down our lives for the brethren.*

– 1 John 3:16 –

Prayer Notes

_____

_____

_____

_____

_____

_____

_____

_____

_____

_____

_____

_____

_____

Lord, Use Me to Touch the Lives of Others

*L*ord, show me what You want me to do today to be a blessing to others. I don't want to get so wrapped up in my own life that I don't see the opportunity for ministering Your life to those around me. Show me what You want me to do and enable me to do it. Give me all I need to minister life, hope, help, and healing to others. Make me to be one of Your faithful intercessors, and teach me how to pray in power. Help me to make a big difference in the world because You are working through me to touch lives for Your glory. May my greatest treasure always be in serving You.

As each one has received a gift,
minister it to one another, as good
stewards of the manifold grace of God.

— 1 PETER 4:10 —

Prayer Notes

Lord, Train Me to Speak Only Words That Bring Life

Lord, help me be a person who speaks words that build up and not tear down. Help me to speak life into the situations and people around me, and not death. Fill my heart afresh each day with Your Holy Spirit so that Your love and goodness overflow from my heart and my mouth. Help me to speak only about things that are true, noble, just, pure, lovely, of good report, virtuous, and praiseworthy. Holy Spirit of truth, guide me in all truth. "Let the words of my mouth and the meditation of my heart be acceptable in Your sight, O LORD, my strength and my Redeemer" (Psalm 19:14). May every word I speak reflect Your purity and love.

Righteous lips are the delight of kings,
and they love him who speaks what is right.

– PROVERBS 16:13 –

Prayer Notes

_____
_____
_____
_____
_____
_____
_____
_____
_____
_____
_____
_____
_____
_____
_____

Lord, Train Me to Speak Only Words That Bring Life

Lord, Your Word says that "the preparations of the heart belong to man, but the answer of the tongue is from the LORD" (Proverbs 16:1). I will prepare my heart by being in Your Word every day and obeying Your laws. I will prepare my heart by worshiping You and giving thanks in all things. Fill my heart with love, peace, and joy so that it will flow from my mouth. I pray You would give me the words to say every time I speak. Show me when to speak and when not to. And when I do speak, give me words to say that will bring life and edification.

Pleasant words are like a honeycomb,
sweetness to the soul and health to the bones.

– PROVERBS 16:24 –

Prayer Notes

_____

_____

_____

_____

_____

_____

_____

_____

_____

_____

_____

_____

_____

_____

Lord, Transform Me into a Woman of Mountain-Moving Faith

Lord, increase my faith. Teach me how to "walk by faith, not by sight" (2 Corinthians 5:7). Give me strength to stand strong on Your promises and believe Your every word. I know that "faith comes by hearing, and hearing by the word of God" (Romans 10:17). Make my faith increase every time I hear or read Your Word. Increase my faith so that I can pray in power. Help me to believe for Your promises to be fulfilled in me. I pray that the genuineness of my faith, which is more precious than gold that perishes even when it is tested by fire, will be glorifying to You, Lord (1 Peter 1:7).

If you have faith as a mustard seed, you will say to this mountain, "Move from here to there," and it will move; and nothing will be impossible for you.

— MATTHEW 17:20 —

Prayer Notes

_____

_____

_____

_____

_____

_____

_____

_____

_____

_____

_____

_____

_____

_____

Lord, Transform Me into a Woman of Mountain-Moving Faith

Lord, I know "faith is the substance of things hoped for, the evidence of things not seen" (Hebrews 11:1). I know I have been "saved through faith," and it is a gift from You (Ephesians 2:8). Help me to take the "shield of faith" to "quench all the fiery darts of the wicked one" (Ephesians 6:16). I know that "whatever is not from faith is sin" (Romans 14:23). I confess any doubt I have as sin before You, and I ask You to forgive me. I don't want to hinder what You want to do in me and through me because of doubt. Increase my faith daily so that I can move mountains in Your name.

Having been justified by faith, we have peace with God through our Lord Jesus Christ.

— ROMANS 5:1 —

Prayer Notes

Lord, Change Me into the Likeness of Christ

*L*ord, I want to be changed, and I pray those changes will begin today. I know I can't change myself in any way that is significant or lasting, but by the transforming power of Your Holy Spirit all things are possible. Grant me, according to the riches of Your glory, to be strengthened with might through Your Spirit in my inner being (Ephesians 3:16). I know that You will supply all that I need according to Your riches in Christ Jesus (Philippians 4:19). Help me to become separate from the world without becoming isolated from it. May Your love manifested in me be a witness of Your greatness.

I have been crucified with Christ; it is no longer I who live, but Christ lives in me; and the life which I now live in the flesh I live by faith in the Son of God, who loved me and gave Himself for me.

— GALATIANS 2:20 —

Prayer Notes

_____

_____

_____

_____

_____

_____

_____

_____

_____

_____

_____

_____

Lord, Change Me into the Likeness of Christ

*L*ord, teach me to love others the way You do. Soften my heart where it has become hard. Make me fresh where I have become stale. Lead me and instruct me where I have become unteachable. Make me to be faithful, giving, and obedient the way Jesus was. Where I am resistant to change, help me to trust Your work in my life. May Your light so shine in me that I become a light to all who know me. May it be not I who lives, but You who lives in me (Galatians 2:20). Make me to be so much like Christ that when people see me they will want to know You better.

*The Spirit Himself bears witness with our spirit
that we are children of God, and if children, then
heirs—heirs of God and joint heirs with Christ.*

– ROMANS 8:16-17 –

Prayer Notes

_____

_____

_____

_____

_____

_____

_____

_____

_____

_____

_____

Lord, Lift Me out of My Past

Lord, I pray that You would set me free from my past. Wherever I have made the past my home, I pray that You would deliver me, heal me, and redeem me from it. Help me to let go of anything I have held onto of my past that has kept me from moving into all You have for me. Enable me to put off all former ways of thinking and feeling and remembering (Ephesians 4:22-24). Give me the mind of Christ so I will be able to understand when I am being controlled by memories of past events. I release my past to You and everyone associated with it so You can restore what has been lost.

*If anyone is in Christ, he is a new
creation; old things have passed away;
behold all things have become new.*

— 2 Corinthians 5:17 —

Prayer Notes

Lord, Lift Me out of My Past

Lord, make me glad according to the days in which I have been afflicted and the years I have seen evil (Psalm 90:15). Thank You that You make all things new and You are making me new in every way (Revelation 21:5). Help me to keep my eyes looking straight ahead and to forgive what needs to be forgiven. I know You want to do something new in my life today. Help me to concentrate on where I am to go now and not where I have been. Release me from the past so I can move out of it and into the future You have for me.

Do not remember the former things,
nor consider the things of old. Behold,
I will do a new thing, now it shall spring
forth; shall you not know it? I will even make
a road in the wilderness and rivers in the desert.

– ISAIAH 43:18-19 –

Prayer Notes

_____

_____

_____

_____

_____

_____

_____

_____

_____

_____

_____

_____

_____

Lord, Lead Me into the Future You Have for Me

Lord, I put my future in Your hands and ask that You would give me total peace about it. I want to be in the center of Your plans for my life, knowing You have given me everything I need for what is ahead. I pray You would give me strength to endure without giving up. You have said that "he who endures to the end will be saved" (Matthew 10:22). Help me to run the race in a way that I shall finish strong and receive the prize You have for me (1 Corinthians 9:24). Help me to be always watchful in my prayers, because I don't know when the end of my life will be (1 Peter 4:7).

But the path of the just is like the shining sun,
that shines ever brighter unto the perfect day.

— PROVERBS 4:18 —

Prayer Notes

_____
_____
_____
_____
_____
_____
_____
_____
_____
_____
_____
_____
_____
_____
_____

Lord, Lead Me into the Future You Have for Me

*L*ord, I know Your thoughts toward me are of peace, to give me a future and a hope (Jeremiah 29:11). I know that You have saved me and called me with a holy calling, not according to my works, but according to Your own purpose and grace (2 Timothy 1:9). Thank You, Holy Spirit, that You are always with me and will guide me on the path so that I won't lose my way. Move me into powerful ministry that will impact the lives of others for Your kingdom and Your glory. I reach out for Your hand today so I can walk with You into the future You have for me.

Those who are planted in the house of the LORD shall flourish in the courts of our God. They shall still bear fruit in old age; they shall be fresh and flourishing, to declare that the LORD is upright.

— PSALM 92:13-15 —

Prayer Notes

_____

_____

_____

_____

_____

_____

_____

_____

_____

_____

_____

_____

_____